She believed she could, but she was tired so she didn't